Contents

Stranding 2

Techniques 4

Stranded Pattern Samples 20

Stranded Hat 26

Stranded Floral Purse.............. 28

Abbreviations 32

STRANDING

Stranding is a technique that involves knitting with two different colors
of yarn per row, which can produce everything from simple to very intricate
colored knitting. The patterns of stranded knitting can look very complicated
in its color changes, but usually only two colors per row are used,
making them look more challenging than they really are.

Techniques

Often people call this technique Fair Isle, but Fair Isle is a type of stranded work, named after the Fair Isle, part of the Shetland Islands.

The word stranding describes what is happening during the color knitting process; the yarns "strand" behind as you work from one color to the next. These strands are also known as floats, and they're best seen from the back side of your knitting.

Stranded knitting can be found all over the world, but it is best known in countries that are colder, because when stranding you produce a double layered fabric that is thick and warm. Typically stranded knitting is done in stockinette stitch, but one exception is Bohus knitting which beautifully incorporates purl texture stitches.

When stranding there are many ways of holding the two different colored yarns; both colors in your left hand, both in your right, or one color in each hand. This is mostly preference, but I think it is to your advantage to use both hands. If you learn to knit using both hands you have the advantage of being able to easily purl with either hand. When you hold both yarns in one hand, the purl maneuver becomes a little trickier and most knitters do not like doing it. If you are always working a knit stitch

(no purls) then you need to knit in the round.

The advantages for knitting in the round (always working a knit stitch) include always working on the right side of your work. This makes it easy to see the pattern or motif, and it eliminates seams. Knitting in the round produces a tube, so if you want to make a garment such as a cardigan, then a steek must be used. This advanced technique is not taught in this book. However, the hat project on page 27 is knit in the round.

The advantage for knitting flat (working both a knit and a purl stitch) is it eliminates the need for steeks. The disadvantage is not seeing the front of your work and for some having to purl. Knitting with both hands makes purling easy with practice. One big advantage of being able to purl is to easily make decorative two-color ribs and decorative textured edgings or to knit Bohus garments. Knitting flat does not mean you have to knit the front and back separately making a seam, garments are usually knit in one piece, so side seams are eliminated.

▲ Front

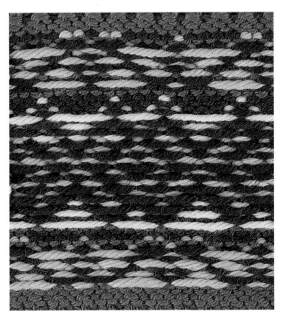

▲ Back

READING CHARTS

Each square represents a color to be knit and the color changes that will occur. The bottom right corner is the starting point and reads across the row to the left. Typically the designs are small and repeat several times across a project. So your chart will have the edge set up area, a repeat area marked off, and maybe second edge area set up if needed.

If you are working in the round, your chart is always read from right to left on each row, but if you are working flat, row 1 is read right to left and row 2 is read left to right.

All charts reflect the garment or project about to be made and how the motif fits within the project. They are often marked for different sizes.

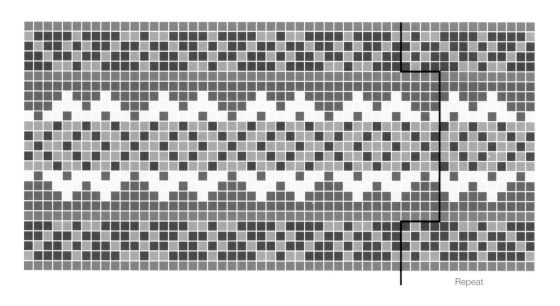

Repeat

Flat knitting

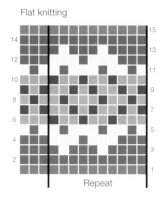

Repeat

Circular knitting

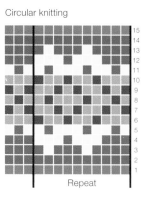

Repeat

Tip: Some chart rows are easy to memorize, but others can be a bit more complex. On these more complicated rows, try to see the flow of what is happening. A lot of patterns have symmetry and once you have worked a repeat or two you will see the rhythm and be able to work across your row without referring to the chart.

LEARNING TO KNIT WITH BOTH HANDS

When learning to knit, most beginners have difficulty holding on to the yarn and getting an even tension. It takes some time before it feels comfortable and natural. So learning to knit with your opposite hand will take practice to become comfortable and achieve an even tension. Remember there are many different ways to hold on to the yarn. Observe other knitters and see the variety of methods.

Knit a flat, one color stockinette swatch with your opposite hand to get a feel and some practice before making a practice swatch of two handed stranded knitting.

Holding Yarn in Right Hand (English or Throwing)

Wrap the yarn around your right hand middle finger for tension, but experiment and see what feels best for you. Your yarn must be able to freely pass through or your stitches will become too tight, and the opposite is true if the yarn is carried too loosely, your stitches will not be neat and tidy. If the yarn is fine, wrap the yarn twice around your finger. For a thicker yarn, place over your middle finger instead of wrapping.

Knit Stitch (white yarn)

1. With yarn in back, insert your needle from front to back into the first stitch on left-hand needle.

2. Throw your yarn from behind up and over the needle, pull through the loop forming a new stitch.

3. Slip the original stitch off of the left-hand needle.

Note: The brown yarn is not visible, but is held in the left hand.

Purl Stitch (white yarn)

1. With yarn in front, insert your needle from right to left in the front of the first stitch on left-hand needle.

2. Throw your yarn down over the needle, pull through forming a new stitch.

3. Slip the original stitch off of the left-hand needle.

Note: The brown yarn is held in the left hand, but is not being used.

Holding Yarn in Left Hand, (Continental or Picking)

Wrap your yarn around your left hand pinkie finger, underneath your ring and middle finger and over your pointer finger for tension. Experiment for what feels best for you.

Knit Stitch (brown yarn)

1. With yarn in back, insert your needle from front to back into the first stitch on right-hand needle.

2. Wrap yarn up and over needle, pull through loop forming a new stitch.

3. Slip the original stitch off of the left-hand needle.

Note: White yarn is in the right hand, but not being used.

Purl Stitch (brown yarn)

1. With yarn in front, insert your needle from right to left in the front of the first stitch on left-hand needle.

2. Wrap yarn down over the needle, pull through forming a new stitch.

3. Slip the original stitch off of the needle.

Note: White yarn is in the right hand, but not being used.

Yarn in Both Hands

After experimenting with your opposite hand and getting a feel for the motion, it's time to try both hands. Do not pull hard on the yarn as you strand them across as this will produce puckering; just let the yarn gently carry across. Spreading the stitches on the right hand needle as you knit will help to keep your tension looser. However, do not be so loose that large stitches are produced.

Get in the habit of using one hand for the background and one hand for the motif. There are a few reasons for sticking with the same hand throughout a project. First, whenever you pick up your project you will not have to think about which hand you have been using and your motions for each hand will become automatic. Another advantage of keeping your yarn in the same hands is your yarns will not get twisted and tangled. In addition, your tension could be slightly different from one hand to the other. If this is the case you would want your tighter tension to be the background and your looser tension to be your motif. This way the motif would stand out more, versus being pulled back into the fabric. I have also heard to use your stronger hand (the one you always knit with when not doing stranded work) on the color that is used the most in the garment or project, which would typically be the background. The method I prefer is the Shetland way, which is to use the left hand for the motif and the right hand for the background. If you watch the path of the two yarns looking over the back of your work, you will see one color travels above which is the right hand and the other color travels below

which is the left hand. The Shetland rule is to use the color that travels under for the motif because it stands out most.

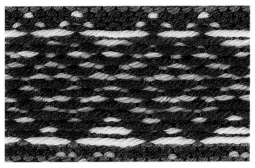

▲ Look closely at the back side of your knitting. The dark yarn is going over, and the white one is going under.

What is most important is to be consistent and carry your yarn in a way that is comfortable and that is as even a tension as you can produce. Every knitter's hand is different, and what works for one person might not work for another. As with all new skills, it could take some time and practice to learn the technique, but the end product is worth the effort. Within a project, always use the same hand positions. If you switch back and forth it will show because of your slight tension differences and because of the path the yarn travels, one above, one below, as stated before.

Tip: If your tension is too tight and the knitting is bubbling, one way to help is to work on circular needles and turn your knitting inside out. The outward curve will give that extra bit of yarn spread and could help with a too tight of tension.

WEAVING OR CATCHING LONG FLOATS

When stranding, sometimes a motif will have many stitches between color changes, and that would produce a long float. How often do want to catch a float? That all depends on your yarn and gauge. The most common number of stitches that you should not exceed is seven stitches or approximately 1" (2.5 cm) of stitches. This is really determined by your yarn choice, gauge, what the project is, and who it is being made for. For example, if you are making a garment for a child, you would not want long floats that little fingers could be caught in. If you are making a pillow, the floats would be enclosed so therefore not an issue, so leave the floats long.

When you weave a float, a small dimple could show on the right side, so take great care to not pull tight the float that is being woven. When you are weaving a float, try to weave it above the same color stitch as the row below.

Weaving long floats on the knit side

Weaving in left-hand yarn (white yarn)

1. Insert right-hand needle into stitch as if to knit.

2. Lift left-hand yarn over needle.

3. Wrap right-hand yarn to knit. Pull through, leaving left-hand yarn. Slide original stitch off needle.

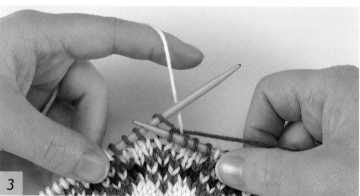

Weaving in right-hand yarn (brown yarn)

1. Insert right-hand needle into stitch as if to knit.

2. Wrap right-hand yarn as if to knit.

3. Wrap left-hand yarn as if to knit.

4. Unwrap right-hand yarn.

5. Pull left-hand yarn through; stitch is made. Slide original stitch off needle.

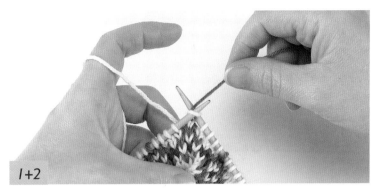

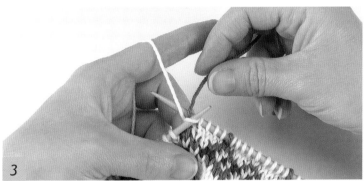

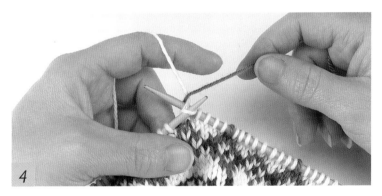

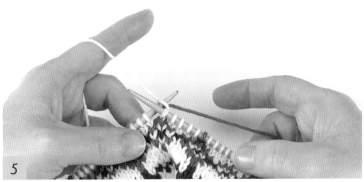

Weaving long floats on the purl side

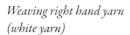

Weaving in left-hand yarn (brown yarn)

1. Insert right needle into stitch as if to purl.

2. Lay left-hand yarn over needle.

3. Wrap right-hand yarn over needle to purl. Pull through, leaving left-hand yarn. Slide original stitch off needle.

Weaving right hand yarn (white yarn)

1. Insert right needle into stitch as if to purl.

2. Wrap right-hand yarn under needle.

3. Wrap left-hand yarn over needle.

4. Unwrap right-hand yarn.

5. Pull left-hand yarn through; stitch is made. Slide original stitch off needle.

EDGE STITCHES WHEN WORKING FLAT

Both colors of yarn need to be attached at the edge, otherwise you will get a small hole. If one of your colors (A) is 4 stitches from the end and it does not get caught at the edge, you turn your work and start stranding and now the next time you use A and it is 5 stitches in. You will have just formed a small spread/almost a hole at that 4 stitch mark, because the yarn did not make it to the edge. The yarn pulled back on itself.

Three ways to catch at the edge

1. Work a float catch at the edge, as described on the previous page.

2. Trap unused color at the edge.

3. If the row you've just completed ends with color A, it is now attached at edge, the next row starts with color B, now it is caught at the edge. Both colors are attached to the edge.

FIXING JOGS WHEN WORKING IN THE ROUND

Just like knitting stripes when you work in the round while stranding, you form jogs. When designing, I try to put the jog in places to make it disappear as much as possible. On the Stranded Purse (page 28), I put the color changes on the edge where the green carries up the entire side. On the X O swatch (pages 24 to 25), the dark vertical stripe in the middle of the X would make a good spot to put the jog, the jog totally disappears or close to it. Sometimes you cannot find a good place to hide a jog, so then I use a jog fix technique. On the stranded hat there is no place to hide the jog, so I did Jog Fix #1 (page 16): sliding the marker over one stitch with each row.

▲ Sliding one stitch over produces an almost invisible jog, only a very slight rise in the stitches can be seen, running from lower right to upper left.

Start of row

◄ This chart shows the Stranded Hat chart doubled up as if it were being used for a pullover. The jog fix occurs exactly as on the hat, but on row 27 the yarns are cut and the jog fix is started over again. The red line shows the path of the shifting row start.

► Reusing the hat chart again, but this time with lots of color! Notice how easy it is to make many small jogs, all at the color change rows (indicated by the red line).

Start of row ▲

I also like to use Jog Fix #2 (page 16 and 17) on my stranded knitting. If you redesign the hat chart into an all-over pattern for a pullover, the design would repeat from the bottom to the top, and if you keep moving the first stitch one over, pretty soon you would be working across the front and heading towards the back of the pullover. A way to solve this would be with each round of a new motif, or colorway, move the first stitch back to the beginning spot. The yarns need to be cut with this method, which would happen anyway if you make a lot of color changes. Another option on a garment is to leave the jog and place it at the side seam. If you are using a fine yarn the jog may hardly be noticeable.

FIXING JOGS

When you knit circularly, you are making a spiral, so the ends of the rounds don't meet but rather continue one stitch higher. There are a few techniques to minimize the jog. If the jog occurs at the side seam of a garment sometimes it is easiest to ignore it. Decide how much the jog offends you. If you are using finer yarn the jog will be less noticeable compared to a bulkier yarn.

Note: All jog fix instructions use a marker for reference to the actions taken, always marking the beginning of the round.

▲ Jog that occurs in circular knitting.

Jog Fix #1

1. *Work one round of new color. At the start of the next round, remove the marker from the needle, slip the first stitch, and replace the marker after the slip stitch.

2. Knit desired rounds. Repeat from *.

The advantage to this fix is all the rows stay the same height. The disadvantage is with every color change the start of the row moves over one to the left. This can cause a slight spiral, and if you have many stripes, the start point could move to an undesirable area, such as the front of a hat.

▲ Jog Fix #1.
Slip stitch highlighted.

Jog Fix #2

I discovered this fix, and made up my own variation, similar to Jog Fix #1. As long as the start of your next color change row does not fall on top of the start of the previous color by 2 stitches (or more), you will not form a spiral. In order not to jog, start your color changes at different points on your knitting, forward and backward.

Your marker does not move, but the beginning of your round does. No matter where the first stitch starts, say two stitches after the marker, when the rounds of striping are done, it will need to end two stitches after the marker, thus making a complete round.

▲ Jog Fix #2.
The first stitch of each color change is highlighted.

1. Knit to the point where you want to change colors, ending at the marker. Slip the marker and the next two stitches. This becomes your new start point, two stitches past the marker.

Note: You could add a second different colored marker to use as you move your beginning points around and keep your original marker to mark your "true" starting point.

2. With new color, knit the required number of rounds, ending at your new start point. (2 sts past the marker).

3. Slip two stitches from right needle back to left needle, you will be back at your marker. The new color can start here at marker or slip the marker and the next two stitches from the right needle back to the left needle and knit the required rounds with the new color at its new starting point.

4. Continue in this manner moving your starting point around. It doesn't matter if you slip 2, 3, or 4 stitches (don't do less than 2), only that you complete your rounds and move your starting points around.

CABLE CAST ON

A wonderful cast on is the Cable cast on. It is decorative and stretchy.

1. Place a slip knot on your left-hand needle. Insert right hand needle into slip knot as if to knit, pull stitch through and place on left-hand needle.

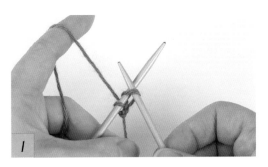

2. Next * insert right-hand needle between stitches, wrap yarn, pull stitch through and place on left-hand needle *, repeat from * to end.

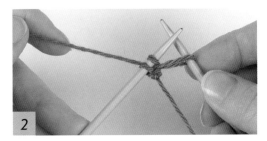

Tip: When using a cable cast on, the first two stitches are a slip knot and knitting into the slip knot, which looks different from the rest of the stitches. Cast on two extra stitches. On your first row of knitting, drop the last two stitches (the slip knot and knitting into the slip knot stitches).

They will unravel without picking the stitches apart and now all the stitches left on the needle look the same. You can use this for flat knitting or for circular knitting. If circular knitting, this area will graft nicely together.

Tip: When working in the round, knit one row flat and then join the knitting. This makes it easier to see if any stitches are getting twisted around the needle. When the garment or project is finished, you can neatly close the opening, matching the slant of the decorative edge. This also works well if you need to put your work on double pointed needles. First cable cast onto a circular needle (any length), knit your first row onto your double pointed needles, evenly spacing your stitches. Join in the next row. This makes it easy to see if any stitches became twisted and will make a neat closure when finishing your project.

THREE-NEEDLE BIND OFF

This bind off is typically used to attach shoulder seams, but in this book it is also used to close pillows, and join the top of a hat.

1. Place stitches to be joined on separate needles.

2. Hold needles right sides together.

3. Using a third needle Insert into first stitches of both needles.

4. Wrap yarn around and pull through both stitches.

5. Slip the stitches off left needles.

Repeat steps 1-5 once more. Two stitches are on your right hand needle. Bind off the first stitch by passing it over the second. Continue in this manner to 3 needle bind off.

MAKING A GAUGE SWATCH

Remember when swatching for your project to use similar needles and the technique you'll use such as circular knit, or flat knit or a combination of both. Adjust your needle sizes if you are both circular and flat knitting in one project and your gauges are different. An example of such a project would be to make a pullover. You would circular knit to the underarms and then continue on your front and back separately by knitting them back and forth.

If you are circular knitting, you can knit a small flat swatch with this technique. Use a circular needle and always work on the front side by cutting your yarns at the edges. Cast on your stitches, knit to end. Cut yarn and slide work to other side of your needles, work across the front again. Continue until you have made a large enough swatch to get a gauge measurement.

Because you are cutting yarns, you cannot unravel and reuse the yarns. Your edges will be loose or distorted, so measure your gauge in the middle of your swatch. If you do not want to cut your yarns, because you might need to reuse the yarn, just let a long float go behind the swatch. Make sure the float is long enough that you can lay the swatch flat for measuring.

GAUGE AND NEEDLE CONSIDERATIONS

Experiment with different needles. If your needle is very slippery, your stitches can fall off a bit too easily, especially if you like to work at the very tips of your needles. If it's too sticky, it's hard to slide your work across your needles. On circular needles it is particularly important to have a smooth join from the cord to the needle because you do not want to stop frequently and push your work over the join.

Your gauge can change from one type of needle to the next, so make sure when you make a gauge swatch you use the same type of needle for your project. Your gauge from stranded flat knitting to circular knitting is often different too. Often the gauge on circular knitting is looser.

YARN CHOICES

Any type of yarn will work for stranded knitting. For a traditional Fair Isle project, a Shetland style wool is best because of its properties. Shetland wool is soft, slightly twisted, and slightly hairy. Therefore, it is easy to steek, cut, and has the ability to gently felt. Wool yarn is often a good beginners' choice, as blocking will reduce tension or bubbling that can occur from pulling yarns too tightly across the back, a typical problem for a newer stranded knitter. Cottons and silk fibers work up beautifully in stranded knitting, but a consistent tension is necessary or else the colors will bubble and not look as nice. These fibers do not have the elasticity of wool, as a result, it will be difficult to fix or block out an uneven tension. A favorite fiber of mine is alpaca because it is soft and drapes well even as the fibers are stranded.

STRANDED PEERIES

Peerie patterns are small repeat patterns, two to seven rows high, used to separate larger motifs like the X and O (page 24). In this case, two are put together forming an all-over pattern.

Multiple of 14 sts plus 9 to center design.
Three colors: A, B, and C.

Follow chart for color changes.

Stranded Peeries Chart

☐ = A
■ = B
▨ = C

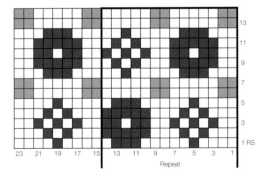

STRANDED DOT

A beautiful, all-over design of dots makes for an exciting pattern. With this array of color, you will have lots of ends. If you made a garment out of Shetland style wool, you could cut the ends and leave them. Another good option is to get two self-striping yarns, one light and one dark.

Multiple of 4 sts plus 2 to center design.
Eight colors: A, B, C, D, E, F, G, and H.

Follow chart for color changes.

Stranded
Dot Chart

■ = A
□ = B
■ = C
□ = D
□ = E
□ = F
■ = G
□ = H

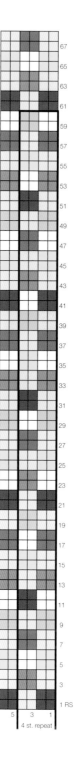

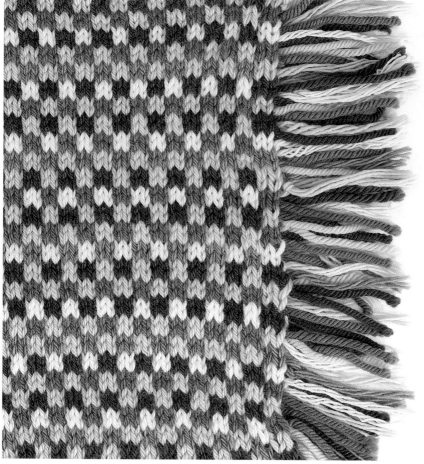

▲ The ends are shown, not to discourage you from making this design, but to make good yarn choices, like Shetland yarns or a self-striping yarn!

STRANDED ANATOLIAN

This design is Turkish and also goes by the name of Rose. The lovely scrolling shape works vertically and would typically be a design on a sock.

Multiple of 34 sts plus 3.
Three colors: A, B, and C.

Follow chart for color changes.

Stranded Anatolian Chart

■ = A   ■ = B   ☐ = C

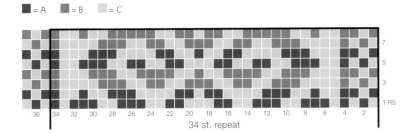

34 st. repeat

STRANDED STAR

Scandinavian stars grace the fronts of many exquisite sweaters. This pattern also has a simple but larger border surrounding the star.

Multiple of chart A (Border): 4 sts plus 1 to center design.
Multiple of chart B (Star): 20 sts plus 1 to center design.
Three colors: A, B, and C.

To make 3 star repeat (as shown) CO 59 sts.
Begin with chart A, then work chart B, finish with chart A.

Stranded Star Chart

- = A
- = B
- = C

Chart A

Chart B

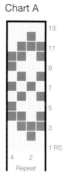

STRANDED X AND O

Common to Fair Isle knitting are many X and O patterns. There are so many beautiful O's it was hard to pick just one, so four have been included. A peerie of ric-rac with dots separates the bands in a subtle way.

Multiple of each square is 32 sts plus 1 to center the design
Six colors: A, B, C, D, E, and F.

Follow chart for color changes.

Stranded X and O

- ■ = A
- ■ = B
- ■ = C
- ▨ = D
- ■ = E
- ▢ = F

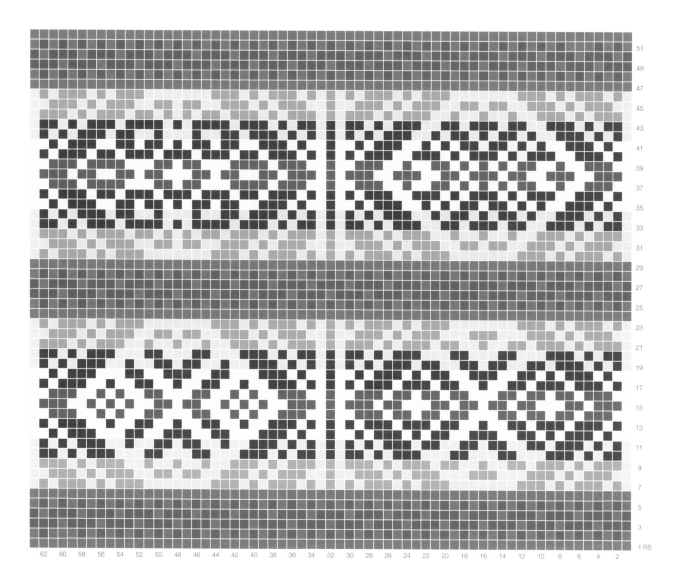

Stranded Projects

Stranded Hat

Simple traditionally styled motif with a contrast edge makes a good choice for a first time circular stranded project. The motif is uncomplicated, making it easy to remember as you knit across the rows. To further aid, an explanation of the best way to hide a jog is included, so you can work through this project with ease.

MATERIALS
#2 Fine/Sport Weight Wool; 225 yd (205 m) each of grey (A) and 22 black (B)

Size 2 (2.75 mm) 16" (40 cm) circular needle or size to obtain gauge

Size 3 (3.25 mm) 16" (40 cm) circular and double pointed needles or size to obtain gauge

Size 4 (3.50 mm) 16" (40 cm) circular needles or size to obtain gauge

Markers

Tapestry Needle

Gauge
25 sts & 32 rounds = 4" (10 cm) in Stranded knitting with size 4 (3.5 mm) needles

Finished Measurements
21½" (54 cm) around the brim × 7¼" (18 cm) high

Instructions

Stranded Hat Chart

■ = A
■ = B

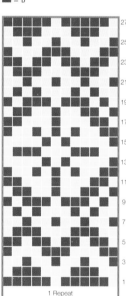

1 Repeat

With size 4 (3.5 mm) circular needle and A, Cable CO 120 sts.

Change to size 2 (2.75 mm) circular needles. Join, being careful not to twist.

With B, work 3 garter st ridges as follows: (knit one round, purl one round) 3 times.

Next Round: Knit 1 row inc 12 sts by *k10, inc 1, repeat from* across, 132 sts.

Next Round: Knit.

Change to size 4 (3.5 mm) needles and work from chart.

Note: in order not to have a jog, slip the first stitch and move the beginning of the round over by one stitch with each round. See reference and chart on page 16 for fixing the jog.

When chart is finished change to size 3 (3.25 mm) needles and St st one row.

Next row decrease 4 sts evenly.

Work straight until hat measures 4¾" (12 cm). If you wish the hat to be longer, then add a few rows at this point.

Cap decreases
Round 1: *K2tog, k6, repeat from *.
Rounds 2 & 3: Knit.
Round 4: *K2tog, k5, repeat from *.
Rounds 5 & 6: Knit.
Rounds 7: *K2tog, k4, repeat from *.
Rounds 8 & 9: Knit.
Round 10: *K2tog, k3, repeat from*.
Rounds 11 & 12: Knit.
Round 13: *K2tog, k2, repeat from*.
Rounds 14 & 15: Knit.
Round 16: *K2tog, k1, repeat from*.
Rounds 17 & 18: Knit.
Round 19: K2tog across.
Round 20: K2tog across, 8 sts remain.

Cut tail and use to thread through loops and close up the hole.

Stranded Floral Purse

This colorful purse will give you practice in both flat knitting and knitting in the round. The purse starts at the bottom edge of the flap, knitting back and forth. When the flap is completed, stitches are added on to form the circular body of the purse. The body of the purse is worked upside down. The bottom edge is finished off with a three-needle bind off.

MATERIALS

#1 super fine wool; 180 yd (164 m) each of pink (A), red (B), fuchsia (C), and green (D)

Size 2 (3.00 mm) 16" (41 cm) circular needle or size to obtain gauge

Size 3 (3.25 mm) 16" (41 cm) circular needle or size to obtain gauge

Markers

Tapestry needle

Gauge

28 sts and 30 rows = 4" (10 cm) over Stranded knitting on size 3 (3.25 mm) needles

Finished Measurements

6" (15.5 cm) wide × 8¼" (21 cm) tall

Tip: On the flap of the purse, cut motif yarn as the color changes are made, and work ends in when finished. On the body of the purse carry the three colors up the edge.

Tip: Usually the motif yarn would be attached to the outside edge stitches as explained on page 13, but because the edges of the purse are exposed, join it to the background stitches right where the motif and background meet: st 3 and st 41 on chart A.

Purse Flap

With size 2 (3.00 mm) needles and D, Cable CO 43 sts. Follow chart for color and needle size changes. Tip: on rows 5 and 6 at the left hand side, use the tail to knit the edge stitches so you do not have to weave the green yarn across the row and back. On rows 38 and 39 add a small piece of green yarn to the edge just like on rows 5 and 6, although it will be on the opposite edge.

Remember to change to size 3 (3.25 mm) needles on row 7 and back to size 2 (3.00 mm) on row 38, due to gauge changes.

Stranded Floral Purse Chart A

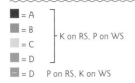

- ■ = A
- ▨ = B
- ▢ = C
- ▨ = D

⎫
⎬ K on RS, P on WS
⎭

- ▤ = D P on RS, K on WS

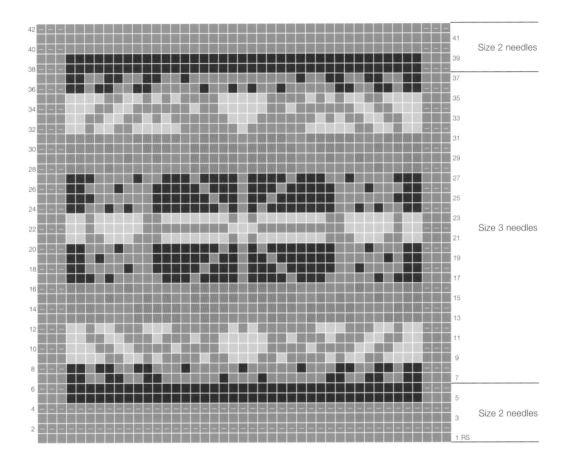

Size 2 needles

Size 3 needles

Size 2 needles

Body of Purse

After chart A is completed you will be on a right side row.

Cable cast on 43 sts and knit across both the new sts casted on and the front flap. Change to size 3 (3.25 mm) needles and join, work chart B two times (the front and back of purse) following color changes.

When chart B is completed turn purse inside out. Put front stitches on one needle and back stitches on another and 3-needle BO (page 19). Work in yarn ends and block.

Corded Strap

Cut 5¾ yd (5.3 m) of 1 strand each A, B, and C, and 3 strands of D. Tie them together in a knot at each end. Fasten one end to a work surface or have someone hold it for you. From the opposite end, twist the cord until it begins to fold back upon itself. Grasp the center, bring the two ends together, and release the center, allowing the halves to twist together. Tie new knots in the ends. Run your fingers over the cord to smooth it out. Sew cord to outside edges of purse, leaving long tails.

Stranded Floral Purse Chart B

- = A
- = B
- = C
- = D

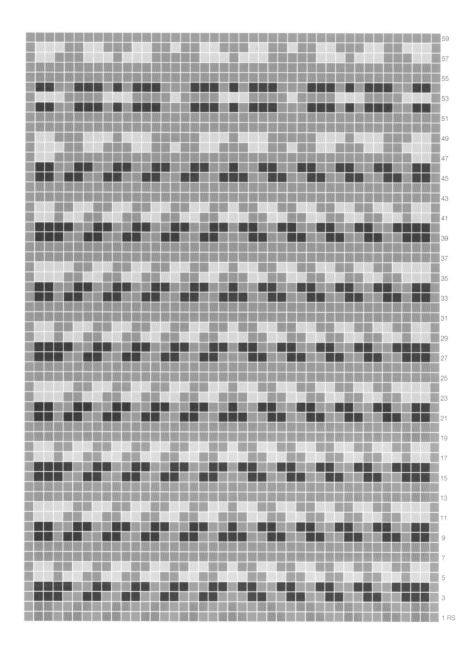

KNITTING TERMS & ABBREVIATIONS

approx	approximate	p	purl
beg	begin(ning)	p2tog	purl two together
BO	bind off	PM	place marker
CC	contrasting color	psso	past slip stitch over
CO	cast on	PU	pick up
cont	continue	RF	right front
dec	decrease	rem	remaining
dpn	double-pointed needles	RS	right side
inc	increase	sl	slip
k	knit	sl m	slip marker
k2tog	knit two together	ssk	slip, slip, knit two stitches together
k2tog tbl	knit two together through back loops	st(s)	stitch(es)
		St st	stockinette stitch
LF	left front	tog	together
M1	make one	WS	wrong side
M2	make two	wyib	with yarn in back
MC	main color	wyif	with yarn in front
m	meter	yo	yarn over